# Random Thoughts of Sleepless Nights

**Poems of Love,**

        **Patriotism,**

**Loss,**

        **and Faith**

## RICH HOGAN, JR.

Written by Rich Hogan, Jr.
Designed and edited by Errol Jud Coder

Dreamscape Publishing

Printed in the United States

10 9 8 7 6 5 4 3 2 1

*October 2019*

ISBN: 9781695872646

I dedicate this Book of my inner most thoughts and love to My Departed Mother Sharon, My Brother Tim, Grandparents Carl, Ruth, and Mary. CHEERS Aunt Nancy! My Mentor and Teacher in High School Mrs. Christine Festine. My Dear Friends in the Scotia-Glenville English Department Mrs. Chant and Mrs. Vernon. To All my USCG Shipmates Especially USCG RAID TEAM VI OIF, 2007 My Family and Good Friends Richard and Jennifer Paszkiewicz and their kids Mal, RJ, Jess!

# Table of Contents

John,

MAY YOU ALWAYS

HAVE PEACE

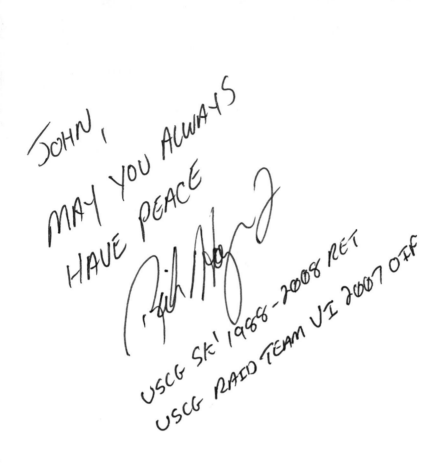

USCG SK' 1988 - 2008 RET

USCG RAID TEAM VI 2007 OIF

# THE
# POEMS

3

# My Wife

I saw you from afar

Your Smile so bright like a shining star

You didn't seem Shy, but you were with another guy

I was getting ready to approach you to see If I could
offer you a drink to buy

The Guy turned and walked away

A drink I order for you and quickly paid

The Guy came back

And I turned away

Your Friend watched me from a distance

She grabbed you and said go get him at her persistence

You caught me before I walked out of the Bar

And you allowed me to walk you to your Car

I asked for your Phone Number

As you sat on your Car Bumper

You Laughed and said No give me yours instead

Almost a Year later we were Wed

On a Rainy Day in April in Your White Dress Walking down the Isle

My Face had the Biggest Smile

Your Father Gave you away as you kissed his cheek

Our adventure we began to seek

It wasn't easy being with me

Others form the outside agreed

You took care of things at home

While I was gone did you feel the same as me alone?

I asked things of you that kept you away for the things you like to do

Many Times, I never Thanked You

Love isn't always about Hugs, Kisses and Holding Hands

It is the Vows we took when we exchanged Wedding Bands

Yes, I was Blessed when the Good Lord
brought us two Strangers together

Now you're stuck with me forever!


## Younger Brother

Just one of many who left this world too soon

I often catch myself looking up at the moon

You and I had a Tuff Life

Our Lives were a struggle a fight

Was it looking for a Parents Love?

Remember the time we got our new Baseball Gloves

I was the Older Brother

You seemed to be always loved and smothered

Did our Uncle, Aunts and Cousins feel sorry for us?

Many Times, we were left alone

For Survival we needed to cut the bone

We hit our Teenage Years and we were on our way

To make our way in this world to make our name

You Succeeded Well You Married and gave me a Nephew

We vowed to each other and in Private not to make the mistakes our Parents Taught us

I Don't blame our Mother and Father or anyone else

I think they did the best especially after their marriage melt

On Paper we were Brothers in life we were friends

Yes, at times I was Jealous and never sought mends

If anyone Picked on you, they were no longer my Friend

I would defend you until the bitter End

People were afraid of me but loved you

And that's the way it was thru our School

I was your Protector, you were my Anchor

We were considered Irish Twins

Your Baseball team always collected the Wins

You Ran Track, Played Football and were a Great Pitcher in Baseball

And at night all the Girls would Call

In our Adult lives we would make each other Mad

Trying to do our Best with Mom and Dad

I'm stuck here without a Mother or a Brother

Trying to reconcile with an unforgiving Father

Please know your always in my heart

Sometimes I wish for us to have a Fresh Start

Your Son is Growing up fast

I know you know that he has your class

Please Guide me in my Mid Life activities

And I will raise a glass to you in all our Family Festivities!

# LIFE GOES ON

As I have made 50 passes around the Sun
The Countdown to my last days on Earth has Begun
Never more apparent as friends start to pass away
You read the Obituary every day
As I attend these Funerals of my Departed Friends and Family
I see the True Love of the Spouse who's life now appears to empty
Sure life goes on but in life with a partner is like a Duet Song
Who sings the harmony when your partner is gone?
Life as you know it is different
Is it true that after one past's the spouse can feel the departed loved ones Spirit?
When does the living spouse begin to heal
After All to death do us part was spoken in the Deal
For a long time the surviving Spouse will wear a Fake Smile

They Spouse will lean on family for a while
Holidays and Family get togethers will never be the same
The Survivors will continue playing the Game
Of Life
Only the Good Lord knows who is next to be called home
And Join our Lord and Savior at the foot of his throne

# Scotia, NY

I grew up in a Small Upstate New York Town

More Like a Village you could hear Traffic Sound

As a Teenager I delivered Newspapers and

Picked up my Bundle at 1$^{st}$ and Vley

I would Fold those Newspapers in the Fog, wind, Rain and Snow as the Moon Rotated By

I would Head down Vley to Second St.

The Early bird customers I would Meet

I would Cross Houston Street to Continue to deliver on Second Street

House Stacked close together made the Job easy on my feet

I would finish Second Street and Go towards Sacandaga Rd to the Corner of 5$^{th}$

Make a U-Turn and Cross Sacandaga Road to Get to First Street almost home so I could Sit

Finish First Street to the Corner of Root Ave.

I would See the Catholic Church and People going to early mass

Once Home I would get ready for School

To Learn the Golden Rule

After School meant Homework or Chores

Which most of the Time I went to the Store

Corino's Market was the Local Butcher Shop

There you could get the Food for Dinner
that was made by Mom or Pop

On Mohawk Ave was Vern's Barber Shop

An old Place where Grandpa could still get a Shave

Across the Street Was Collings Park where we would play

Wintertime meant Sledding Down Collings Hill

July meant Fireworks from Jumping Jacks

on a quiet Mohawk River Still

Fishing in the Spring on Collings Lake with your

Friends after the Winter Thaw

We were underage and didn't break any fishing Laws

Wiffleball Games being played on the Vley Road Alley where Mets
Fans Played Yankee Fans for Bragging Rights

We were Boys and settled things with Fights

Lathrop's Pharmacy is where we dropped our

Prescriptions when we had a Cold

Pick up your Scripts before 9:00PM after that the Store was Closed

Lathrop's had 2 Locations Corner of Vley Rd and 5<sup>th</sup> Street, And on the Main Drag of Mohawk Ave.

If I remember correctly their prices weren't that bad

I worshiped at Our Redeemer Lutheran Church

On Sundays I would wear my best Ironed Shirt

Some of my best times were riding my bike all around the town

Looking for a School Yard Football Game
or any other activities around

One of my all-time Favorite Part Time Jobs was Working at Lorenzo's Pizza after School and on Weekends

Lorenzo's was closed on Sundays so that was a Day
I could hang with my Friends

I remember the Day I left the Village September 26, 1988 My Dad and I departed our 21 Washington Ave Upstairs Flat

In 8 Weeks, I was going to be coming Back

That September Day I departed for U.S. Coast Guard Basic Training in Cape May, NJ. I was now an Adult and had to Start a Career

My Dad wasn't going to let me sit around he wanted my Brother and I get our Lives in Gear

During Basic Training my Shipmates talked of theirs homes with Great Glory

I would patiently wait to Tell them of Scotia, NY and My Story

The Day I graduated Boot Camp I was full of Pride

I couldn't wait to Sit in the Ride

That would take me Home on Leave

I Walked off that Plane and Many Didn't Believe what they see

It Was me!

My Hair was Shorter and waistline Slimmer

When I was back many Relatives and Friends
invited me over for Dinners

17 Days Later I was back at the Albany Airport this Time in Dress
Uniform having to say Goodbye

It Stung to leave and with many tears in my Eyes


# Another Goodbye

This Goodbye was going to be awhile because
I was reporting to the Fleet

In December in Albany it was raining a light Sleet

I reported Aboard my First U.S. Coast Guard Cutter

The First Call Home was to my Mother

I Worked and saved up Money for Leave

I couldn't wait to get home so my Friends and Loved ones in Scotia, NY.,
could See Me!

As I grew older and proceeded with my Adult Life Scotia, NY
was always in My Sights

I will Call Home often and got the News the Babe Ruth Field
got Night Lights

I have taken my Family down the Many Streets of Scotia
or as I call Memory Lane

Still filled with pride and Never with Shame

Sadly, my trips back home is not only for reunions or Fun

I attend Funerals of Old Friends and Family Members whom I spent with in
Scotia under the Bright Sun

I also attend Weddings and hook up with ole friends and Family talking
about the Glory Days

Just like everyone my age I know time has caught up and taken its toll and
my Hair is getting grey

Now when I go back to town, I must wear Glasses
I drive by the High School and Remember my Favorite Classes

As my memory gets to Fade
May I always remember the Days
Of my Time in Scotia!

# SMILE!?!?

I find no inner Joy the Fire seems to be barley lit

I Can't make a Happy Smile not even for a Little Bit

If my Smile does appear please know it was you that got me there

And if you happen to smile with me, we will share

When the Smile is gone Know it will disappear

I don't want your Pity, or feelings that you care

Please move on and don't get wrapped in my despair

I would hate to drag you along in my feelings of sadness

If you try to make sense of me It will drive you to Madness
I'm a walking Black cloud

My Mind is Sound

Just keep going and remember the smiled we shared

And remember it's my sadness to bear

## A SIMPLE GRAVE AMONGST MANY OTHERS

Well the First week of March is in the Books I left
Jacksonville to head North

I have more Training in Washington D.C. But I have a long Weekend
a Friend I must See

He is no longer among us, but many Think of him Daily

A Nobel fight with Cancer he fought very bravely

It's hard for me to know he is gone the Battel he fought was so Long

He even rang the Victory Bell

The Cancer Treatments put him thru hell

I'm not sure if he was ever Cancer Free

If he was it came back rapidly

A late Sunday Morning as I headed into church

A phone number that never calls and I felt the Worst

I was told our Hero, Mentor and Friend was Dead

He was home and passed away in his Bed

Everyone in the Company knew the Arrangements

But as often do Work, and Life got in the way I wouldn't be able to Make the Engagement

I know for me this Friend I must See

I seek closure this I need

He Is a Marine buried in a Field full of Heroes

As he was placed in the Ground those that were there heard the Rifle Barrels

21 Gun Salute is what Ross earned

They Could smell The Gun Powder as it Burned

TAPS Played as Friends and Family wipe away Tears

Later that Day I Raised my Glass of Beer

To our Friend and Brother Ross

We still feel your Loss

# ON BEHALF OF A GRATEFUL NATION

Crowds of Veterans Stand at Attention

At the Passing of a Veterans Funeral Procession

On its way to the Veterans Final Resting Site

This Country is Free Because of this Veterans Might

Fought for this Country on Foreign Land

The Honor Guard Readies Its Rifle Hand

Ready, Aim. Fire Shouts the Command

The Honor Guard Responds with Unwavering Hand

As the Shots Echo Throughout this Sacred Land

Veterans at Attention Raise Their Right Hand

As the sound of taps flows thru the land

Veteran Brother and Sisters Holding Hands

Knowing what was done for this land

To be free

The Flag is folded for all to see

And presented to the Family

On Behalf of a Grateful Nation

Your Veterans Service and Dedication

We offer you this Flag for their determination


## Father/Son and the Damage Done

It's very hard to love when there has been hurt and Pain

I'll will understand if I go Insane

I cried so much when my Mother Left My Father for another Man

Our Days were over for our Family to walk in the Sand

My Father really did his best to provide for us Kids and the things we needed for a Living

I longed for a Fathers love he needed to be giving

He worked 3<sup>rd</sup> Shift and did time in the Air National Guard

The Living he had chosen was hard

He provided for us so many times

Many Times, his Kids Put him in a Bind

He was a single Father who made ends meet

A Second wife was hard for him to seek

He did get us a Stepmother

But he had Secrets as a Father

You see there was Beatings towards us Kids many times I was the Oldest, so I got what he had to give

I can't imagine the Pressure he was under to pay the Bills and put a roof over our head

During those beatings I wished he was dead

As I have gotten older, I learned of PTSD from his days in Vietnam

That 1 Year in Country made part of his mind gone

It wasn't till I went to War to know what he felt

That's when I realized the Cards that were dealt

My Father has Since Found God and his Lord and Savior Jesus Christ

I try to Love but I still have a Fight

I have a Hard time giving and showing him a Son's Affection

Many Times, I roll my Eyes when he wants my Attention

He says He loves me all the Time

My Reply puts me in a Bind

I love but I hate

I still do what a Son needs to do to take care of his Father, but I feel like a Snake

I wonder if he knows the Struggle, I have towards him

And if he were to ask Where would my Story Begin

Yes, he rescued My brother and I from a Childhood Trouble

In the end I reply with "I love you to Dad" but it's muffled

## Farewell Mother

I will never forget that Hot August Day

I received the News you had passed away

I didn't know how to react

A long time I braced for the Impact

You had been sick for far too long

Somedays I wished you were already gone

Hearing you on the phone in constant pain

Again, I wish the Lord would take you away

When I went to see you at your wake

It was way too much for me to take

I your first-born son and I broke down

I didn't care who was around

Time seem to stand still

Every Passing Moment I became more Ill

I was tasked as a Paul Bearer

I was the Last to touch what was your forever

The Lowered the Casket into the Dirt

At this point you would no longer hurt

For God had finally answered my Prayer

And his love for you was a comfort and a care

It hasn't been easy with you not walking this earth

After all it was you that I met after the birth

I was your First-Born Son

That could never be undone

I was surrounded by Family I didn't know

Time was passing so Slow

I wanted to get away from your Grave

And to just fade away

When I was alone, I had time to reflect

Thru you 56 Years we had our ups and Downs, but you were the Best Mother this Son could expect

# My American Flag

As a Kid I placed my Hand over my Heart and said the Pledge of Allegiance Every Morning Before School Starts

I never gave a second thought of the Various Parts

In the Pledge

As I got older, I understood the Words I Said

I have seen the Stars and Stripes Riding high in the Sky

I seen it lowered to honor those who died

The Red on our Flag is a Symbol of the Blood that was shed

The White stands for the Purity and Innocent of our Kids as we kiss them Goodnight in Bed

Our Children Can Sleep at night knowing somewhere a Solider Stands a Watch all day and night

That Soldier stands ready to Fight!

For my Freedom.

The Blue is for the Hope of the New Start

You can't achieve the American Dream if you don't do your Part

Many Around the World hate the Red, White, and Blue

Every Day our Pledge isn't said in a Majority of our Schools

Yes, We Have that Freedom to choose

If you take God and the Pledge out of our Schools, we as a Country
Will Loose

It truly is sad to see the Americans who take for granted the Gift of
Liberty

By Burning my Flag in Protest in our American Cities

I kindly ask that before you Torch my Flag you give a second thought

A thought for all those who gave their life and Fought

Under the Flag you hate so much!

## Questions to Start your Day

Did you grow up in a Ghetto?
Did your Dreams ever find you walking in a Peaceful Meadow?
Did your dreams ever fall short
Or did an outside influence bring you Hurt?
What if you had total control of another person's mind
What would you do to help Mankind?
Would you go after your own thoughts and dreams
or create harm to those who were mean
Would you go to a Stranger and give them a Hug when they needed it
Or, would you be selfish and say forget it!

Today too many are self-absorbed in the way they wish to live their
life

They will do anything in their might
to Prove that they are Right even if they are wrong
When they do finally see the Light is it too late
If you done it too long You my Friend must accept your fate

The Best part is that You as a Human can restart and rebuild to a better way
God Gave you Life to start a Brand new Day
Don't let your next chance Slip away!

## Soul on Loan

I have seen the dead enemy of my Nation and felt no remorse.

Could this Enemy be the apocalyptic Black Horse?

Revelations talks about the "End Times" which I believe are happening this day

We as God's Children need to Pray!

We don't wish or want the Mark of the Beast

I and my fellow Christians want to join your table at the Great Feast

At what Cost will a Christian Pay
Remember Jesus died for you his life he gave
Will you recognize the Number of the Beast?
If you Don't Your Lord and Savior you will not meet
Everywhere you look is the Devil at Work
Wants of Flesh, and Money he will come with a Smirk

He will whisper it's Ok and your Soul you just gave away
Remember you are SAVED!

There are no gimmicks to Gods Word
The Good News You Must Have Heard
If you Haven't Grab Gods Book
Open the Pages and Take a Look

There is no Hidden Code
You will not be left alone
Accept Jesus in your Heart
Share his Word Do your Part!
The Soul You save may be your own
For your Soul Belongs to God right now it's with you on Loan

# Fight or Flight

I don't look forward to the nighttime for me it means Sleep

There is a constant movie playing in my head that I don't want to Keep

No matter what plays out in the night

I know it will mean fight or Flight

I see friends, Family and enemies from my Past

Like a Hollywood Director from a Movie I must Cast

There is no specific to scenes in my Dreams

Many a Night I wake up in a Scream!

Sometimes I dream of bringing People in my life back

Other time I'm out in front leading an Attack

No matter what plays out

I started before it ends with a Shout!

Did you ever dream of something so scary?

You wake up in a panicked Frenzy!

Sometimes in my Dreams I see my own Death

But my Lord and Savior I haven't met

I see myself at my Burial Site

No one there to morn for me which causes me freight

No family, Friends are around my Grave Site

What did I do to suffer this Plight?

All I can see and hear is the wind as it whispers thru the air and stirs up the leaves

Seriously no one grieves!?!

Morning approaches and the alarm clock sounds

A new day is upon me and my feet hit the ground

I kneel and pray to the Lord in the Heavens above

All I have ever wanted in this life was to be loved

I put on my working clothes and walk to the Driveway

In 10 Minutes of headed to work I will be on the Highway

I will sit at my desk and everything will be Normal

All my clients that day I will greet and be formal

The Drive home after this 8 Hour Plus Day

I will need a nap and hit the hay

I know this is Wrong

I hit the pillow humming a Song

Day turns to night

I relive the fight or flight

# My Boys

I'm curious of what my 2 Boys Think of me

I vowed I would never make the Mistakes my Father did you see

My Oldest Boy is Strong and Independent and Takes After his Mother

My Youngest just moves along but really loves his Brother

I do things with my Kids that my Father never did with me but what
do I have to prove

I'm a Father and their Troubles I try to sooth

Yes, I failed but not taken them Fishing as I should Have

But they have done many other things for which they are glad

The Oldest as I chased my Career became the man of the House at a
Young Age

Sometimes we butt Heads and he has Fits of Rage

As I get older, I know my Time is Short they have lives of their own
and the time I have with them left Hurts

I will send invites for concerts or Ballgames

But their lives move on with others and I feel ashamed

I just must let go so they can grow and prosper

To me that would hopefully make me a Good Father

# Inner Peace

Give me a Moonlit Night and a quiet still River

I Love the Summer Heat and how it makes me shiver

There is so much Peace and Quiet at Night

The Frogs and Animals searching for food by the Moon Light

I love the calmness of a Bobber sitting in the water and the action it makes
with a Fish hits the Bait

I set the Hook will the Fish Escape?

I really like sitting and listening to Tunes on the Beach sitting in my chair

If you see me, you know at this point I don't have a care

Many Thoughts run thru my mind on these quiet nights
and it suits me just fine

I get mad when the Sun starts to shine

That means my Night is over and time to start a new Day at Work

Time to get Dressed and Put on my Company's Polo Shirt

As I work thru another day

I think of things that might get in my way

From me sitting on the Shore and throwing out that Bobber one more time

When I make that Cast at night, I feel Fine

One More Time on the Shore and Believe me this is what I live For

You See that Fish got away and I need to even the Score

# Friend

It's been a year since you have gone

Most of the World has moved on

It's not that easy for some of us

We still feel as though we were hit by a Bus

Still Pictures of you in our Head

Fill our dreams as we go to bed

At the Functions that you and I used to attend

sits an empty Chair reserved for my Friend.

Every now and then I take a glance at the Empty Chair

Just to see if my Friend Gary is Sitting There

Legs crossed at our meetings

Handshakes to a New Days Greeting

Your Careful Steps as you honored are Prisoners of War and Missing in Action

A bright Fall Day Dressed in your Army Alphas

Your White Gloved Hands as your marched to Amazing Grace

That dedicated Look you wore on your Face

The Slow Salute of Honor to our Fallen Heroes

Was channeled thru you from your time on the Battlefields

You never retired from your Military Life

You reached out to others so they could have a better life

You lived the America Dream with your Wife and Kids

And later in life you were blessed with Grandkids

It was easy to notice from a far

How all in your Circle gravitated to you like a Rock Star

You were easy to work with you knew wrong from right

If anyone challenged, you they were in for a fight

I know of no one other than your Wife

Who had the Highest integrity?

And that's how you lived your life

Those who knew you, knew it would hurt when your gone

But the memory of you comes back like a favorite song

Yes, my Friend this Year hasn't been easy

I kept my Promise to you and that is what has helped to ease me

## HOMELESS VETERAN

They were discharged with nothing to do

The Demons of their tour started to come thru

Drugs and Alcohol was the crutch

This put them in a terrible rut

They lost everything to include their self-respect

Those who loved them became upset

They left to hide their shame

Deep inside they knew they were to blame

Living under a bridge in their struggle and doubt

All they could do was SHOUT!

How do we better ourselves how do we seek help?

How does one get back to oneself?

They look in the Mirror to face their addiction

Some get help from an Intervention

Some vow never to use again

Others lose in the End

Those who do survive take heed

Because they saw their friends pass before thee

They Enter the Program to become Human Again

Not all will pass the Test

But those who do will surely be blessed

They will go and start a new life

With Hope and Promise and no addiction Strife

They will reunite with family and friends

And ask for one final Forgiveness from them

They will rejoin society

As they try to maintain their Sobriety

Off into the World they will flow

There Past is what they must let go

No more will they be Homeless or have to hide their shame

They will rejoin the ranks of being a Veteran with no Blame

They will pass on what they learned

To prevent others from getting burned

This will be their gift back to Society

Thanks to the Lord Almighty!


## "Kneel Before My Savior"

I went and Served Uncle Sam

Took the oath, raised my Right Hand

Fought the Enemy Tooth and Nail

Only to be prisoned in PTSD Jail

Sought Help for my Condition

Only to be denied by a VA Decision

You Need to Appeal the VA Rep Said

Who keeps appealing when you're dead?

I can't Work because of my Disease

Good Lord Take Me Please

I Shout and Cry at Night

Only to be Locked up and sheltered in the Light

How can I continue to live with this Situation?

Who wants to live in Isolation?

Reached Out for my Battle Buddy's Help

Only to find he killed himself

I'm a Warrior I have my Pride

I won't go like others died

Fall to my Knees

Dear Lord, Hear Me Please!

## Through Green Eyes

I wish I could un-see the stuff that I have seen

This World is cruel and mean

Nightmares at night of me spinning thru the air

It's very tuff for one man to bear

Cries at night come and Go

The night creeps by very slow

I do have physical Scars the ones I received were once covered by
Band-Aides

Daily my Mental Health Needs First Aide

Help is not seeked or sought

Times, I wish I never Bought

In my Dreams are cries for Help that are real

The Devil is watching to see if my Soul he can Steal

I wake up not wanting to move

But Daily things I must do

My Hurt is from head to toe the Drugs they give
me make me feel like hell

Out the Door I go I Put on my protective Shell

Interactions with those who have the same afflictions

Many of whom suffer from some type of addiction

I must put on a Warriors Brave Face

Theirs stories and mine I wish to escape

I don't hold God responsible for the things I've seen and done

I'm just thankful my faith doesn't require me to grab that "Gun"

You see it's so very easy to exit this life

But it's hard to do because you don't want to hurt your Wife

I'm not so concerned with what others my say

I just need to take life day by day

Is there any solace for what these things I feel?

Remember the Pain for me is Real

I wish to live and see the developing of my Kids

And for them not to do what I did

Yes, I lived a life of sorrow

Tomorrow is another day God will let me borrow

I don't believe this is a Path that I choose

Many who have gone down this path will loose

I will stick to my Christian Faith

I won't sub come to the Devils Bait

Here I sit and pray Daily

Know the Lord has Guardian Angels to Protect me failing

## Salty Chief

My Friend was taking his last Walk across the Brow,

He Gave Me a Salute he was Heaven Bound

He told me to brush those Tears away He loved the Life God Gave

I remember how he told the Glory of His U.S. Navy Stories

And how he found the Perfect Wife who gave him the Perfect Life

Throughout the Years there were Laughter and Tears

As he helped raise his children, he took away their fears

He was proud of his kids and the accomplishments they did

Some of his kids worked in the Private Sector while others chose a
Military Adventure

One thing that was constant in his life was the love he had for his wife

He had high respect for his fellow Man

If you were his Friend, He would say call me Dan

His love for our country was to be admired

Peace for our Country is what he desired

I will always remember his Friendly Handshakes

And I will look for him at the Pearly Gates

In the Navy he was a Chief Storekeeper

On Land he was a Husband, father and Friend

When our time is over, he will meet us on the other end

At that Point I will return my Salute to my Friend and Shipmate Dan!

## Gentle Giant

I knocked on the Gentle Giants Door

I looked thru the Window and saw tears on the floor

I looked in the Driveway and saw the Black Harley was Gone

I zipped up my vest

I headed West to look for my Buddy Les

On that overcast day something in my gut told me
bad was coming my way

The Sky Turned Grey as our Gentle Giant passed Away

A Phone Call Came to Me A number I hadn't known

A Friend had told me Les Went Home

I can't comprehend what you just said please repeat

......and I heard the Words Les is Dead

I looked to the Sky and said a prayer for my friend

I just saw him how this could be the End

Less than a Week before his Service

I was asked to prepare his final chorus

How do you Honor a Gentle Giant who gave so much?

For me saying goodbye was and always has been tough

I stood there and directed the tribute and ceremony

As I told the Story of Les saying in Lieu of Flowers Send Money

In the End Les didn't care that he was gone

He is at the Lords Table Singing Songs

He wanted what was best for the Veterans he cared and Rode for

That his last selfless Act

was to always give Back!

# A ROUND OF FEAR

There isn't much to say as I drink the Day Away
What Pain do I hope to erase what will be my Great Escape?
As I order another Drink my soul begins to shake
I know it's Wrong but I want the Pain to be gone
Inner struggles and second guessing life's choice
In my Head are loud voices
Do you wish to live or die
Pack your Stuff and say goodbye
If I live what then do I do this again?
I don't want to hurt nobody other than myself
Thoughts in Head are Cloudy and fogged in doubt
Another Sip of Whiskey I take It's my choice and mistake
I'm not surrounded by Love only those who choose this life of Death
Slowly I wither away surly this pain must go away
My Glass is empty time for another Round of Death I Drink down
Thirst isn't quenched as I suck in another Breath
Why is life take forever?
What will my Part in life be will I be the Drunk in the Family
Will I be the punchline of many Jokes?
Will they say those mean things to me before I croak?
I Don't want Pity as I wither Away Get out of my life I didn't invite you to
stay!
The Time has Come God's will, will be Done
My Family will most likely attend my funeral and Bury me in the Family
Plot
Isolated in the Back by overgrown trees that are ready to rot
My Drunks at the Bar will sit and raise a glass to a life that had gone way to
fast
It wasn't easy this road of Life I took Guess What nobody was surprised or
Shook
Yes, even as I'm lowered in my Grave People shake their heads and talk
about the disappointment I gave.
It will be hard to rest in enteral peace for no one wants my soul to keep!

# GOLD STAR PARENTS

It wasn't always easy being with me
But what you get is what you see
I have Friends and family waiting for me on the other side
Now, I will get to see them, I hope you don't mind
I was chosen to go first because you could better manage the hurt
During my Service in the Armed Service
I met many a Men and Women who shared the same purpose
To Protect our Country Right or Wrong
We received orders to Attack at Dawn
My last Will and Testament signed
My Signature on the dotted line
We went in Hard, Ready, and Fast
Only to be sent in the Air by an IED Blast
Upside Down and Looks and feels of Slow Motion
Outside the Humvee is a lot of commotion
As I wait for help I begin to Yell
Get me out of this Living Hell!
I look to my left and my Driver is Dead
I then feel the Blood flowing from my head
The Ringing inside my Head and the dimmished fading eye sight
I black out and see no more day light
I wake up and I don't know where I am
I hear English and hope I'm in my Homeland
Tubes and Machines keeping me alive
I'm in and out of sleep and then I flat line
The Family is notified that I died
Many will have Cried
The Price of Freedom is a Loved one's Blood
The Day is Raining and my final resting site is uphill climb in the Mud
TAPS is Played and Mom and Dad get a Comfort of many Hugs
The Now Join the Club
They are now Gold Star Parents in my Hometown

This is where I grew up and played now buried in the Ground
On the Mantle in my House lies an American Flag Folded and on
Display
Along with the Purple Heart and Bronze Star For the Freedom that I
help gave
Meanwhile there still isn't any Peace with the War that I was killed in
The Gold Star Parents list forever increasing

# My Soul to Keep

Hello, Dad it's me your Son
I wish to apologize for taking my own life with your Gun
You and Mom gave me everything I wanted in Life
I just didn't have what it takes to Fight
I can tell you clearly this wasn't the easy way out
But no one can hear me with a gun in my Mouth…...

Instantly, I become a Lost Soul
There I'm on the Floor Getting Cold
It seems like hours before someone found my remains
By Now the Blood stains
On my Clothes and the Ground
Many People Gather Round
I see tears in the Eyes
Of Strangers looking to the Sky
Asking Why?
By now My Soul is further away
A Police Officer Walks up my Walk way
My Parents are at the Door
I can feel my Parents Stomach hit the Floor
The Officer removes his Cap and tells the news of my Death
Both Parents Wept
What seems forever doesn't really take that long the Officer turns as

Momma Cries my Baby's Gone!
But for me my Soul is damaged in Eternity
The Pain I put my Parents thru will destroy their unity
Out of all this is just one Certainty
I'm Dead!

# Ode to Rich and Jen

I Wrote Poem for my two Dear Friends Rich and Jen.

They started dating in High School and have been t
ogether ever since then

They were married on a Beautiful September Saturday in 1994
Gods Love was cast upon them for Sure
As all things in life we buried Family Members and Friends who
attended that Blessed Union
As the Plan for their Family was to get bigger a house they needed to
find and be Moving
The First Offspring was a Beautiful daughter Named Mallory, next
was RJ, and the Baby of the Family was Jess
The Grandmothers were blessed I would venture to Guess
Rich and Jen went into Full Parent Mode
Dance Class, Horse Lessons, Baseball, Bowling, Field hockey,
Basketball always on the Go
Jen Cooking in the Kitchen with culinary delights
Meanwhile Rich and Jen are reefing the Kids Fights
Milestone Achievements for the Kids and School Projects hanging on
their Castle Walls
Many Band aids , hugs & Kisses when their children
would trip and Fall
The Girls Selling Girl Scout Cookies
Rich and RJ Building his car for Pinewood Derbies
Many a late night to complete Science Projects
Only to go to the Bathroom at night and step on Legos and other
Objects
Weather they wanted it or not The Paszkiewicz Castle was the Kids
and their friends Hang Out Spot

Always open doors and Kids Running in and Out adding and
subtracting to the Flock
Sleepovers and late invites to Dinner
Rich Wondering if the Miami Dolphins will ever be a Super Bowl
Winner
The Kids are now or getting ready to go to college
To seek and Gain Knowledge
Rich and Jen getting into their Twilight Years
Comfort is Found for the two of them on a Patio Drinking Beers
Jen is Planning her next getaway to Salem, Mass
Meanwhile Rich is looking for the
next Grateful Dead Music Festival Bash
25 Years has reached them and us pretty fast
I think they know in each other's Heart their Marriage will Last

Made in the USA
Monee, IL
28 February 2020

22418329R10026